How to Train Your English Mastiff

A Step-by-Step Expert Guide to Grooming, Caring, and Raising a Giant Breed Dog from Puppy to Adult to Behave Positively

Finnley Crestwood

Copyright © 2024, Finnley Crestwood

All rights reserved. No part of this publication may be reproduced, distributed, or transmitted in any form or by any means, including photocopying, recording, or other electronic or mechanical methods, without the prior written permission of the publisher, except in the case of brief quotations embodied in critical reviews and certain other noncommercial uses permitted by copyright law. For permission requests, write to the publisher at the address below.

Disclaimer

The information in this book is intended for general guidance on training. It is not a substitute for professional advice. Always consult with a veterinarian or certified dog trainer for tailored recommendations. The author and publisher disclaim any liability for actions taken based on the content of this book.

Finnley Crestwood

How to Train your English Mastiff

BONUS:
20 English Mastiff dog Homemade Food Recipes

A Step-by-Step Expert Guide to Grooming, Caring, and Raising From Puppy to Adult to Behave Positively

Contents

Introduction — 9

Chapter One — 13

Understanding the English Mastiff — 13

Origins and history — 13

Physical Characteristics — 15

Temperament and Common Traits — 17

Chapter Two — 21

Preparing for Your Mastiff Puppy — 21

Puppy-Proofing Your Home For a Giant Breed — 21

Gathering Essential Supplies and Vet Care — 24

Vet Care & Emergencies — 25

Finding a Reputable Breeder — 27

Chapter Three — 31

Bringing Home and Bonding with Your Puppy — 31

Preparing for the Pup's First Days — 31

Establishing a Schedule & Routine — 34

Positive Reinforcement and Crate Training   36

Crate Training Perks   38

Chapter Four   **41**

Potty Training a Mastiff Puppy   **41**

Understanding Challenges With Giant Breeds 41

Establishing a Routine & Preventing Accidents 43

Using Confinement When Unattended   45

Chapter Five   **49**

Socializing Your English Mastiff Puppy   **49**

Introducing Your Puppy to New Sights, Sounds and Dogs   49

Teaching Important Commands   51

Managing Jumping, Nipping & Mouthing   53

Chapter Six   **57**

Loose Leash Walking Training   **57**

Understanding the Basics of Loose Leash Walking   57

Training Exercises for Calm Walking   59

Harness, Head Halter, or Martingale Collar
Options									61

**Chapter Seven									65**

**Advanced Obedience Training & Commands
65**

Settling and Relaxation Protocols					65

"Wait," "Leave It," "Come" & Emergency Stops
67

Extending "Down," "Sit" and "Stay" Duration	69

**Chapter Eight									73**

**Managing Mastiff Puppy Biting and
Aggression									73**

Root Causes of Biting and Aggression				73

Positive Reinforcement Methods to Curb
Nipping									76

Techniques for Handling Possessiveness			78

**Chapter Nine									81**

**Exercise Requirements and Environmental
Needs									81**

Exercise Needs By Mastiff Life Stage				81

Playing, Walking, and Hiking With Your Mastiff

Safely 84

Summer and Winter Weather Precautions 86

Chapter Ten **89**

Grooming & General Care Essentials **89**

Coat Brushing, Nail, Dental and Ear Care 89

Bathing Techniques & Dry Shampooing 91

Car & Plane Travel Tips 92

Chapter Eleven **95**

Feeding & Nutrition Requirements **95**

Caloric Needs By Life Stage 95

Preventing Bloat Risk 98

Chapter Twelve **101**

Health & Medical Care **101**

Recognizing Signs of Common Major Health

Issues 101

Budgeting for Healthcare Costs & Pet Insurance

Options 103

Adapting Home and Routine for Aging Dogs 105

Special Bonus 107

20 homemade food recipe ideas for English
Mastiff with ingredients and preparation
instructions 107

Introduction

Few dogs can stop traffic like a 230-pound English Mastiff ambling down the street. These massive yet gentle giants turn heads with their sheer mammoth size and imposing presence. But what many don't realize about this intimidating ancient breed that once battled Roman legions and lions for entertainment is that inside beats the loyal heart of a sensitive companion. Rather than attack dogs as stereotyped, Mastiffs aim only to please their people.

I discovered this firsthand many years ago when my girlfriend surprised me with an adorable floppy-eared Mastiff puppy for my birthday. As we raised our sweet Murphy from an uncoordinated bundle of wrinkles into a trained gentle giant greeting guests with a thumping tail and smile that looked more like an Elvis Presley snarl due to heavy jowls folded over his teeth, this special breed completely won me over.

But raising Murphy to be a model Mastiff citizen with skills improving our daily life together didn't happen through sheer luck or chance. His sheer size alone at 110 kg (240 lbs) meant if he didn't learn basic manners, he could easily bowl over elderly relatives, small children or some of our petite friends with just an affectionate nuzzle. Dragging me down the street like a ski sled whenever a squirrel caught his attention would make our neighborhood walks disastrous. And the soon-to-be leather loveseat we picked up at a flea market would rapidly resemble shredded beef jerky once his puppy chewing phase kicked into high gear if I didn't teach what things were off limits to nibble.

Luckily through consistent positive reinforcement training tailored to Murphy's needs each step of the way from floppy pup to mature companion, this lovable Mastiff exceeded my expectations in responsiveness and picking up cues - with just the right motivation. As with many giant breed canines bred historically to work independently guarding estates, English Mastiffs respond best to training prioritizing relationship development through play, praise and enticing treats rather than scoldings or correction. Guiding them with benevolent leadership allows their natural devotion and desire to please to shine through.

Within these pages, I share the proven modern force-free training techniques I discovered while raising Murphy stem not from battling or breaking a dog's spirit through intimidation as traditional mindsets once promoted. Instead, motivation-based methods build communication, understanding and mutual respect between Mastiff and guardian leading to better behavior from these peaceful beasts.

Whether you're considering adding one of these good-natured giants to your home for the first time or a seasoned Mastiff owner encountering new challenges with an adolescent dog entering their "teen" phase, the diplomatic strategies and tailored tips ahead empower you to train YOUR English Mastiff positively. While their towering height and muscles conjure up ferociousness, don't be fooled - with relationship-centered guidance focused on your bond rather than brute strength, even novice owners can cultivate obedience in these teddy bears and unlock their ultimate loyalty. Just be prepared for big doses of drool and fur ahead while changing perceptions about misunderstood gentle giants along your journey together!

Chapter One

Understanding the English Mastiff

Origins and history

The English Mastiff is a massive, old breed with a long and storied past, and it stands tall and proud. Because of their enormous stature and aristocratic demeanor, mastiffs are among the most easily identifiable canines. But what were the beginnings of the guardian breed we know now?

According to researchers, the Mastiff first appeared in ancient Assyria, Persia, Babylon, and Tibet more than five thousand years ago. "Canis mastinus," meaning "guarded dog" in Latin, is whence their name originates. Predators and dangerous humans were fended off by these canine ancestors as far back as 700 BC. They were so massive that they could easily defeat any predator. The current English Mastiff can trace its ancestry back to the massive molosser dogs brought to Britain by the Roman troops during their subsequent invasion.

The nobility were the only ones allowed to own Mastiffs in medieval Europe. The breed became a status symbol in manors, escorting aristocrats and guarding estates from intruders or thieves. Their wariness towards outsiders and intense protectiveness were invaluable before modern security and police.

In 1835, when dog fighting was declared illegal, the Mastiff fell out of favor in England. After decades of decline verging near extinction, a devoted group of breeders recovered and stabilized the Mastiff in the late 19th century utilizing stock from the English countryside. Specimens like Champion Crown Prince and Champion Candidate became progenitors for today's Mastiffs.

The breed earned international recognition and imports to the US began by the late 1800s. The AKC initially recognized the Mastiff in 1885. Today's English Mastiffs retain instincts for guarding yet make for peaceful family companions and show dogs, with over 500 puppies registered yearly. Their pedigree extends back millennia as one of the most important Molosser canines in many other huge breeds.

Physical Characteristics

Instantly recognizable for its sheer gigantic size, the English Mastiff displays a noble, dignified demeanor. They're considered the heaviest breed on average, despite height ranges of just about 30 inches.

Head: The Mastiff's huge head is a unique characteristic, with a black mask reaching a broad back cranium. The skull is square and the forehead creases while awake. Muzzle form is square, broad, and deep. Eyes are medium large, dark brown, and placed wide apart. Ears hang near to cheeks.

Body: Powerful, muscular yet ponderous body built for strength over speed. Equal body length to height. Shoulders and front legs thick-boned, forelegs set straight. Firm-level back and broad chest for lung capacity. Tail high set, reaching hocks when erect.

Coat & Color: Short dense double coat with straight, coarse outer hairs incorporating apricot, fawn, or brindle markings over a black mask on the face. Long-term health issues such as hip dysplasia, bloat, and cancer are concerns due to their massive mass.

Despite their fearsome presence, English Mastiffs are gentle giants with moderate exercise needs. Their quick growth as puppies necessitates good nourishment and a gradual rise in physical activity. Care is essential in hot weather to prevent overheating. Though tough to physically maneuver, they can thrive in most residential conditions.

Temperament and Common Traits

Beneath the brawn of England's renowned guard dogs is the heart of a devoted companion and family member. Though discipline and socialization are necessary because of their guardian heritage, Mastiffs tend to be calm, loyal, and eager to please given their ancestry. However, ownership involves consideration of a few anomalies...

Laidback: Mastiffs are enormous couch potatoes comfortable with a couple of daily walks. Short bursts of play and modest exercise keep these easy going pets pleased without extended yards or jogs.

Devoted: These dogs bond intensely with primary caretakers, reflecting their single-family estate past. Separation anxiety is frequent if left routinely alone. They'll follow you from room to room to be near.

Generally Calm: With early orders confirming you're the leader and ample outside time, Mastiffs are gentle dogs unlikely to charge fences or tackle strangers without strong provocation. Proper introductions to unfamiliar persons will prevent misunderstandings.

Stubborn Streak: Mastiffs can be tricky to inspire for training. But positive reinforcement, especially with delectable goodies, promotes focus for brief sessions. Consistency keeps children from ignoring commands they don't enjoy mastering quickly.

Heavy Shedding: Be prepared for dog hair tumbleweeds with their dense double coat! Regular brushing helps maintain loose hair and promotes new growth.

Expensive to Feed: Budget for costly high protein food for these huge breeds require through puppyhood and adulthood, easily $150 or more monthly.

Though their sheer bulk is daunting, English Mastiffs want to please their owners. With proper training and early socialization offering guidance, these dedicated guardians use their brawn for good rather than harm. Patient-experienced owners will discover a peaceful yet fun-loving companion.

Chapter Two

Preparing for Your Mastiff Puppy

Puppy-Proofing Your Home For a Giant Breed

Before an English Mastiff pup enters your life, sufficient preparation of your home environment and lifestyle is essential. At maturity, Mastiffs can weigh over 200 pounds—that's a LOT of cute puppies wrecking potential havoc in a limited space! Beyond standard puppy-proofing, take these extra steps to set up your house for large breed safety:

shut Access: Use baby gates and pens to shut off rooms and areas of the house. Allow access only when you directly oversee and train acceptable chewing and toilet behaviors. Confine them till house manners improve.

Remove Temptations: Get down on your puppy's level and examine for attainable dangers. Eliminate loose electrical cords, hazardous houseplants, prescriptions, minor choking risks, and valued objects you can't risk being chewed.

Reinforce Furniture: Wrap crates around the table and chair legs. Stabilize unsteady shelving that may get bumped and toppled. Consider placing valued breakables out of wagging tail range during the clumsy puppy era.

Install Safety: Add safety latches to kitchen cabinets containing poisonous cleansers and avoid rodent poisons that appear like attractive snacks to explorative dogs. Secure trash cans to prevent dangerous chewing and intestinal obstructions.

Adjust Storage: Keep food bags, kitty litter, and other tempting chewables inside rubber bins out of reach. A metal storage cabinet gives added safety so cunning paws can't break in.

Prep Potty Space: Set up an indoor potty area with a cage, pads, and cleaning materials so you can continue housetraining if the weather doesn't cooperate for outdoor trips.

Reinforce Doors/Walls: Protect door edges and drywall against nail scratches and impact damage. Use corner guards, metal shields, or plywood as an economical option to replace drywall later.

Evaluate Landscape: Scan your outdoor environment for safety threats - hazardous plants, pharmaceuticals, fertilizers, or chemicals kept inappropriately. Restrict access to balconies or steep drop-offs. Fence yard if possible.

Giant puppies grow FAST. Take measures early before behaviors become set habits. Patience and prevention now save tremendous frustration and expense down the road!

Gathering Essential Supplies and Vet Care

When prepared for the Mastiff puppy's arrival, stock up on supplies needed for health, comfort, and training during all life stages. From leashes to gates to vet fees, being ready BEFORE they arrive home streamlines a good transition in those first important weeks.

Must-Have Supplies:

- Extra large box with room to grow - Two strong-duty leashes and collars with ID tag info
- Stain remover enzyme cleaner

- Heavy ceramic food bowls to withstand tipping - Variety of chew toys for teething relief - Treats for positive reinforcement training - Grooming supplies include nail clippers, dog brush and toothbrush

Handy Extras:

Consider a huge dog car harness, elevated bed frame, puppy gates, poop bags, and indoor potty tray for stressful situations like illness or harsh weather when outdoor toilets aren't viable. Invest in stain-proofing your furniture and car seats early too!

Vet Care & Emergencies

Any new dog needs a reliable veterinarian for frequent preventative care. But a huge breed notably relies on informed direction regarding nutrition, weight, bone growth, and other features impacting lifelong mobility.

Before they arrive home, develop a relationship with clinics experienced in large dogs. Discuss realistic expenses. Budget roughly $400-500 for first vet checks, immunizations, preventatives like deworming. Spay/neuter will cost $200-300 at roughly 5-6 months old. Annual care like checks and vaccines run $200 per year.

Save an "emergency puppy fund" for anticipated concerns like illness, injury, allergic reactions, and intestinal obstructions from swallowed things. These demand rapid medical care and are expensive considering large puppies' increased drug dosages and recovery challenges. Consider pet insurance plans early on or be ready to charge $1000 or more.

Never compromise on a growing pup's core veterinary needs – the investment actually pays health benefits years down the line!

Finding a Reputable Breeder

Avoid supporting unscrupulous large scale breeders churning out Mastiff litters for profit without genetic testing or breed preservation in mind. Seek responsible small hobby breeders focusing on temperament, health, and function over appearance.

Red Flags to Avoid:
- Constant litters of pups always available
- Will ship puppies unseen
- No third party verified health certificates for parent dogs
- Unable to provide references from former puppy owners

Ideal Breeder Traits:

- AKC English Mastiff breeder of excellence, member of a Mastiff breed group
- Only produces 1-2 litters per year from own personal dogs
- Certifies hips/elbows ratings, thyroid, cardiac health of sire/dam
- Socializes pups to different sights/sounds for eventual behavioral stability
- Provides help & take-back guarantee if concerns emerge later

An ethical breeder interviews buyers too, to ensure their homes suit the needs of large breeds. They worry about where pups end up. Be prepared for contracts mandating spay/neuter, vet care, and return of the dog if you can't keep them.

Patience pays when the appropriate breed ambassador enters your life! Establish ties with breeders and vet early, ask questions, and visit new litters. Budget realistically, then the joys exceed the problems of welcoming an English Mastiff!

Chapter Three

Bringing Home and Bonding with Your Puppy

Preparing for the Pup's First Days

The day you take your Mastiff puppy home signifies the start of a lovely friendship. During the adjustment time to their new home, utilize these techniques to build your bond up for long-term success:

Puppy Orientation

- Take your pet on a tour of accessible places first, keeping it positive if they feel overwhelmed. Reward calm behavior with praise or treats.

- Introduce house rules and boundaries right away. Redirect using toys while chewing improper stuff.
- Use a command like "easy" if play gets too rough, then divert energy to a game of fetch.
- Play crate introduction games with rewards so the place feels like a safe den when you leave.

Manage Solo Time

- Young pups need virtually continual monitoring so don't leave them unmonitored for hours. Start gradually with minutes alone then utilize baby gates to constrain access while you have me-time.
- Provide intriguing toys packed with rewards in the playpen or kennel when you step out. Frozen Kongs keep pups happily busy for over an hour!

Reassure at Night

Whining from isolation distress is common the first few nights. Try keeping the crate near your bed to minimize anxiety and resist overly consoling so they don't grow dependent. Draping blankets over the box can further muffle stimuli and create a warm den feel.

Prevent Accidents!
- Puppies need to be eliminated extremely regularly, so proactively take them out every 20-30 minutes when roaming and shortly after eating, drinking, playing, napping, and nocturnal crating.
- Tether them to you with a leash so you may monitor for circling, sniffing, or crouching actions and run outside. Accidents generate more accidents if the odor stays!

Welcoming an English Mastiff puppy establishes the groundwork for your future adventures together! Stay patient, attentive, and cheerful throughout the opening weeks and you'll have a great start to a lovely new chapter.

Establishing a Schedule & Routine

Giant breed puppies rely on predictability and stability. The key to molding healthy conduct is an established daily schedule matching their basic needs. Follow this schedule for happy puppyhood:

Morning Merriment!
- Take puppy potty right after waking up. Offer strong compliments and allow them a chance to completely eradicate.
- After potty, engage in low-key indoor play or chew time.
- Serve a nutritious breakfast in periodic intervals. Pick up after 10 minutes.

Learning Ventures
After breakfast, proceed outdoors for a sniff 'n learn to walk displaying them car sounds, objects, etc. Use this opportunity to practice attention

commands with high reward rewards. Come back for more play & training.

Nap Intervals

Like babies, young pups grow physically and mentally during quality daytime sleep. Enforce naps in the darkened crate for 1-2 hours, adding an extra afternoon sleep till 5-6 months old.

Afternoon Antics

Schedule another toilet break, play session, a short walk, and free access to toys or chews following naptime. Continue reinforcing training principles learned that morning.

Calming Evening

As nightfall nears, serve dinner then ease stimulation with soft snuggles or massage. Take a final pottie walk then let them settle in the open crate with a stuffed chew toy as you unwind until bed.

Night Night Ritual

Take one last toilet trip soon before bedtime. Settle the dog in the crate near your room overnight. Use a keyword like "night night!" so they learn to wind down.

Follow this constant pattern addressing biological needs and your Mastiff will continue evolving into a placid, well-adapted companion all through puppyhood.

Positive Reinforcement and Crate Training

Raising a gentle behemoth like an English Mastiff depends on promoting positive habits far more than scolding errors. Use rewards-based training to develop an unshakable link.

Understanding +R Positive Reinforcement (+R) hinges on rewarding desired behaviors so they increase in frequency long-term. For pups, make training look like play by limiting sessions to under 5 minutes. To implement +R effectively:

- Get the pup's attention with a pleasant, cheerful voice - never angry. Say their name, kiss noise, or flash a toy.
- Show and lure to prompt the behavior instead of manhandling into positions. Guide them with food until offering the behavior autonomously.

- TIME your "yes!" reward marker phrase immediately as the pup does the right thing, followed swiftly by a high-value food treat.
- Randomly reinforce successful repeats later with praise or scratch break instead of food so it sticks long term.

Crate Training Perks

A crate suiting your Mastiff's size needs to serve several reasons beyond confinement when you leave. Benefits include:

- Den-like safe spot to withdraw and relax - Transportable "bedroom" for overnights or vacations - Potty training accelerator since pups won't soil their bed - Barrier to danger when you can't supervise them - Recovery location after medical procedures or injuries

Use +R for Positive Associations
Introduce crating slowly so they learn to appreciate their crate, and not dread getting "locked up." Scatter treats around, near, and inside the open door, praising as they investigate the rest inside. Practice brief crating intervals after fun when ready to pass out. Use stuffed chew toys just for the crate.

Soon, they'll relax and self-soothe when locked within.

Patience and rewards-based training ensure your beloved Mastiff respects you as a fair, trusted leader. Keep sessions cheerful and end on a pleasant note if concentration wavers. Your link will continue getting stronger when your pup chooses outstanding behavior because it feels good, not due to intimidation. Stay dedicated!

Chapter Four

Potty Training a Mastiff Puppy

Understanding Challenges With Giant Breeds

English Mastiffs grow so rapidly as puppies that housetraining creates particular obstacles. Understanding why they differ from small dogs helps develop a plan setting them up for success.

Physical Limitations

Bladder capacity expands as your Mastiff puppy grows. They can only manage cravings approximately 1 hour per month at first. Large breeds also usually take a bit longer to physically coordinate elimination.

Clear Communication

These gentle giants want to please but can't naturally link their preferred bathroom locations without precise guidance. You must teach the right spot, reinforce immediately, and minimize faults through management.

Motivation & Distraction Challenges

Mastiffs favor resting over training! Remaining aware and responsive demands encouragement. Additionally, their protective instincts can override toilet cues when distracted by sounds or strangers.

Environmental Factors

Larger dogs have higher waste volumes and take longer to relieve themselves. Inclement weather, new locales, or loud environments can further hinder removal.

Have realistic expectations. Active supervision, confinement when unattended, and positive reinforcement are crucial foundations for adjusting to problems large breeds confront on the journey to being housetrained.

Establishing a Routine & Preventing Accidents

Prevention is the key to Mastiff pup potty training success! Follow a predictable schedule prompting toilets in defined areas to reduce indoor incidents.

Designate Relief Areas

Pick an easy-to-clean place like a porch or patio near the entryway. Always take them to this place on a leash using a trigger word like "Go Potty!" and reward quickly when they are eliminated.

Predictable Feeding

Adhere to a consistent scheduling of meals and measure servings properly. Rapid bone growth depends on sufficient dietary intake. Record when they eat, drink, and excrete to find natural bio cycles for appropriate potty times.

Learn Early Cues

Puppies sniffing in circles, suddenly ceasing play, or waking from naps need to go out. Until a schedule is established, proactively take them every 30-60 minutes plus shortly after confinement, dinner, play, and nighttime.

Supervise Constantly

Tether your pup to you inside so you can divert and hurry them out the moment they signal a desire to eliminate. Utilize crates and pens when unable to actively focus. Accidents cause more if the odor remains.

Patience Over Punishment

Clean accidents using an enzymatic cleaner. Scolding encourages hiding elimination out of fear - not the purpose. Just interrupt softly with an "uh uh!" and then rush outdoors to demonstrate the appropriate spot.

Using Confinement When Unattended

Prevent mishaps and damaging boredom when commitments call you away from home. Use confinement, food puzzles and chew toys to set your developing Mastiff - and your stuff - up for safety and success. Here's how:

The Right Size Space

Crates should allow standing, turning, and laying down. A pen permits sleeping, pads, and water close. Dogs naturally avoid soiling their den which buys you more time.

Meeting Needs First

Walk the pup, let them relieve themselves fully outside, provide mental + physical stimulation beforehand, and offer a stuffed chew toy to distract them when alone.

Gradual Independence

Start solo times are relatively short. Reward calmness, then utilize planned errands to deliberately lengthen the duration of confinement and prevent separation distress.

Positive Associations

Randomly toss treats and praise your pooch in the pen so they don't solely link it with your leave. Make it a soothing refuge.

Patience Over Punishment

As with potty training, kindly redirect any unwanted behavior but never discipline crated/confined pups or they'll reject future confinement.

With planning, prevention, and positive reinforcement, house training your English Mastiff puppy prepares them to thrive as part of your family. Stay mindful of needs, motivated by prizes, and devoted to consistency!

Chapter Five

Socializing Your English Mastiff Puppy

Introducing Your Puppy to New Sights, Sounds and Dogs

Early positive exposures in a controlled situation decrease future reactivity and animosity when meeting new stimuli. Tailor these mastiff puppy socialization tactics to develop confidence:

Invite Visitor Dogs

 Arrange one-on-one polite greetings with neighbor pups up to date on shots/preventatives to eliminate illness risk. Keep leashed, allowing mild sniffing if both appear comfortable. Reward calm conduct profusely on both sides.

Exposure Outings

Carry snacks on neighborhood walks to alleviate anxiety when meeting autos, bicycles, schoolkids etc. Pair with a cheery tone and reward relaxed responses. End on a good tone before the pup gets terrified.

Puppy Classes

Controlled group classes offer safe exposure to novel venues and other puppies. Focus on connection development over obedience drills. Classes shouldn't reach 6 months old.

Positive Vet Visits

Occasionally bring your puppy by the clinic for weights, goodies, and praise without an assessment to create familiarity around handling, equipment, and the building itself.

Prioritize Socialization

Introduce diverse stimuli and canines inside the vital prime socializing window under 4 months old when most receptive to establishing lifetime confidence.

A continuous stream of good encounters now minimizes troublesome aggressive or scared feelings later. Tailor socializing to your developing pup's needs.

Teaching Important Commands

Life skills like swift recalls and impulse management help keep exuberant big-breed dogs out of danger. Build these must-know behaviors early:

Come

Use an enthusiastic, encouraging tone and high-value gifts anytime you speak your pup's name or "come!" Guide back to you with the lure if needed. Throwing a reward party ensures they'll listen next time too.

Leave It

Hold a treat in your fist and say "Leave it." Give stronger goods on the other hand the soon they cease nibbling your fist. Gradually practice with food on the floor, then toys and inappropriate chew items.

Drop It

Say "give" and offer a substitute prize as you expose your open hand. Bribe with food under their nose if resistant. Always deal; never take something away violently.

Stay: Ask for a sit/down first, say "stay," take a few steps back, return, and reward before they move. Very gradually aim for prolonged stays before releases and celebrations.

Watch Me

Capture their eyes naturally first. Later say "Watch me!" to promote eye contact then deliver a stream of little prizes as long as they keep attention on you.

Use high-incentive gifts, pleasant energy, and brief sessions to motivate your Mastiff puppy during continuous basic training. End politely and try again later if attention wavers. They'll rapidly master these key habits on cue!

Managing Jumping, Nipping & Mouthing

Giant paws and keen teeth demand considerable training to manage but never punish normal playing behavior in growing pups. Here's how to curb roughhousing:

Channel Energy Redirect jumping or nipping into a training session or fetch activity instead of scolding. Meet their physical and mental needs proactively.

Reward Alternatives

Trade a chew toy when they nip skin, rewarding gently once they hold onto that instead. Teach them how you desire them to use their mouths.

Discourage Gently

If they jump up or mouth too hard, say "Easy!" in a severe tone or stand immobile folding your arms and ignoring them until four paws are on the floor. Then praise.

Reinforce Sitting

Ask for a sit before offering attention, food, toys, or letting passage through doorways or gates so they don't barrel through jumping.

Persist with Patience

Puppies explore the environment using their teeth and paws without realizing size or force. While continually redirecting, know this exhilaration will fade with maturity directed by your leadership.

Raising a stable, trustworthy huge breed like the Mastiff requires robust socialization foundations that establish confidence to manage novelty, along with impulse control training to short-circuit natural eagerness. Put in the work today for an ambassador canine kid can be proud of!

Chapter Six

Loose Leash Walking Training

Understanding the Basics of Loose Leash Walking

Before going into mastiff leash training tactics, grasp the ultimate purpose and issues their great size presents:

What is Loose Leash Walking?

Loose leash walking keeps your Mastiff awake you without pulling, blazing ahead, or falling behind. There should be a "J" loop in the leash from your hand to the pup's collar. The goals include:

- Walking peacefully by your side or near behind in heel position
- Immediate sits at curbs before crossing streets
- Loose leash for the bulk of a walk vs continuous corrections
- Ability to modify pace and direction without opposition

Challenges with Giant Breeds

English Mastiffs can exceed 200 pounds at maturity. Their height and power require very motivated training to accomplish abilities like heel and loose leash walking. Specific challenges include:

- Distraction overload reduces focus in stimulating environments
- Heavyweight dragging forward or laterally on leash
- Tendency to surge ahead and get the next smell/sight first

- Lagging if they decide they're done walking
- Easily startled by severe corrections that put huge dogs down

Set your Mastiff and yourself up for loose leash success by increasing engagement with you on walks using rewards and friendliness. Control the situation to prevent poor habits from forming too.

Training Exercises for Calm Walking

Use these mastiff-friendly conditioning drills to reinforce awareness, impulse control, and heel abilities for calm pack walks:

Precision Feeding

Before walks, spread a piece of their kibble in the grass for them to scent out. Occasionally call their name and ask for a sit before dumping more handfuls. This action stimulates their brain, preventing frustration.

Silky Leash Game

In low distraction circumstances, brace the leash with one hand an inch from the pup's muzzle and pass a cloth ribbon leash portion through the other, prompting them to target and grip it. Reward with primary leash slack. Release/repeat. This builds self-control.

Red Light, Green Light

Randomly vary the pace, call the pup's name, and exclaim "Slow down!" to prompt slack leashing up behind you. Reward with praise and treats. Or after a few steps, exclaim "Beep beep!" and hurry forward to inspire keeping up without tugging. Fun pace modifications increase response.

Gradual Distraction Exposure

Increase environmental challenges very carefully, initiating leash sessions in quiet regions at off-peak times with a small room to explore at first. Stay inside their stress threshold while rewarding check-ins. Up criteria over weeks.

Correcting Pulling on the Leash

Despite proactive engagement training, hyperactive adolescent Mastiffs may still reach the end of the leash when recognizing mice or arriving dogs. Here's how to curb pulling:

Harness, Head Halter, or Martingale Collar Options

Try equipment putting control near the pup's center of gravity such as front attach harnesses or head halters led by the muzzle. These devices minimize pressure on delicate growing necks if they lunge without violent modifications.

Be a Tree

When they pull, promptly halt moving and stand like a "tree," keeping slack in the leash. Wait for the dog to come to your side enquiring what's wrong before rewarding the slack leash generously and starting forward again. Repeat many reps.

Positive Reinforcement

Coax back to heel position using a cheery voice, food, or fun toy as soon as the leash is taut, then praise and carry on. Frequent rewards for preferring to walk close to you motivate corrections.

Turn and Walk the Other Way

Change course abruptly so they have to rush back into an acceptable heel position if they start to forge in front of you. Reward after they catch up into place then restart your intended course. Keep them watching you.

Stay focused on basic skills preventing future problems through relationship-based training. Keep lessons concise, enjoyable, and ending on successes to enhance your English Mastiff's confidence thriving on a leash!

Chapter Seven

Advanced Obedience Training & Commands

Settling and Relaxation Protocols

Before difficult skills, cultivate tranquility and impulse control foundations utilizing these relaxation techniques:

Capture Calmness

Note when your Mastiff lays down voluntarily. Say "Good settle!" and toss treats to reinforce the action without pressing it. Soon they'll start giving calmed-down postures looking for rewards.

Mat Training

Place a special mat in heavy traffic areas. Lure the pup onto it with food, praise the minute their belly touches, and treats for remaining. Gradually the build mat stays up to 30 minutes disregarding interruptions.

Relaxation Cues

Pair a verbal hint like "Chill out" or motions like extended kneel stroke with praise and rewards when they relax on their own. It becomes a trained "off switch."

Moving Settles

With mat training accomplished, occasionally lift the mat a few inches while the pup is settled. Reward sticking out. Very gradually demand remaining relaxed on the mat while you hold or move it around the room.

These foundations promote impulse control, length, and distraction resistance for sophisticated acts including courteous greetings, long stays, and pedestrian safety skills.

"Wait," "Leave It," "Come" & Emergency Stops

Mastering these fundamental obedience guidelines keeps your Mastiff out of household mischief and safe off-leash if needed:

"Wait" at Doors/Gates

Before leaving or entering, ask for a sit. Open the door/gate slightly, and say "wait!" Return to reward if they hold the seat instead of speeding through. Very progressively increasing wait duration before releasing.

Proof "Leave It"

Gradually boost requirements after they can avoid clutching food, toys, and chews on cue. Practice with new enticing items, throwing gifts on the floor at pet stores, and outside distraction training.

Instant Recalls & Emergency "Come"

Randomly call pup every five minutes anytime you're together at home with an urgent tone and big prizes. Sprinting to you and prompt sits must develop an entrenched habit, one they'll revert to when summoned in difficult situations.

Emergency "Stop" or "Down"

Choose a distinctive danger signal like "Stop!" and pair it with dropping a packet of prizes away from the hazard once mastered. High distraction proofing can train auto-downs if they ever go toward highways. It may save their life!

Although eager to please, English Mastiffs can have an independent streak demanding consistency reverberating across training in all circumstances for true reliability when it matters most.

Extending "Down," "Sit" and "Stay" Duration

Gradually condition patience and impulse control for complex, lengthy behaviors like stays:

Break It Down

Ask for brief sits and downs first. Quickly return, praise, award. Over several reps, add a "stay" command, take one step back, return, and release. Very carefully extend distance and duration.

Challenge Attention

When solid, occasionally stroll to the end of a lengthy line, call their name, and bend your knees. Immediately reward running over and sitting in front. Sending the message of arrival always pays off more than breaking stays.

Switch Locations

Generalize stays in all rooms of the home, then low-distraction outdoor settings, then more stimulating destinations for brief durations. Vary surfaces like tile, grass, and even playground equipment.

Fade Lures & Rewards

At first, always lure into an appropriate position with a gift. Over time, the phase removes lures until obeying voice cues independently before rewarding stays. Then begin periodically rewarding with praise instead of food.

Make It Fun!

Toy plays, surprise gifts flung between paws, or chase games after release stops make duration labor fun. Always release with marking phrases like "okay!" after staying.

Motivate your Mastiff for permanent steady stays by incremental measures boosting criteria appropriate to their desires. Persevere through common adolescent distraction phases for a trustworthy partnership.

Chapter Eight

Managing Mastiff Puppy Biting and Aggression

Root Causes of Biting and Aggression

Unpleasant biting and aggressive actions in Mastiff puppies must be redirected, not punished. Understanding the source helps identify relevant training. Common explanations include:

Normal Teething Discomfort

Mouthing and nipping increase at 4 months old as puppies begin losing baby teeth for adult ones. Swollen gums hurt and they chew for relief. Gentle bite inhibition training helps them learn to ease up.

Poor Impulse Control

Like hyperactive youngsters, puppies usually play too exuberantly, jumping and nipping without grasping their size and power. Calmness signals, enforced naps, and limiting overstimulation aids enhance self-regulation.

Fear Periods

Between ages 6-14 weeks, and then 6-18 months, puppies go through heightened sensitivity to stimuli that can trigger defensive biting. Avoid overexposure until their confidence stabilizes.

Lack of Exercise

Puppies develop a craving for active play and exercise. Lagging on their requirements causes unrestrained, unrelenting mouthing and roughhousing due to bottled-up energy and tension.

Prevent this by sufficient daily activity adapted to their age.

Medical Issues

While rare, suffering from orthopedic issues, infections, parasites or injury could elicit severe reactions typically out of character. Vet exams help rule out contributors to behavioral changes.

In most circumstances, approval, consistency, and meeting puppy requirements lessen biting and animosity in adolescent Mastiffs. But the next portions present appropriate training approaches just in case.

Positive Reinforcement Methods to Curb Nipping

Even without meaning harm, a huge puppy's razor teeth can wreak devastation. Transform biting into relaxed mouthing via rewards-based training:

Provide Acceptable Chews

Redirect biting onto durable chew ropes and toys. Praise quiet chewing and shove food within to make correct outlets especially rewarding over hands and clothing. Rotate novel toys to prevent boredom.

Encourage Gentle Mouthing

When puppy fangs meet skin, say "Easy" in a calm voice. Praise once jaw pressure softens, continue the game. Over time kids understand soft mouthing keeps play going, not harsh biting.

Withdraw Attention

If a nip occurs during a loud game, rise up discreetly, terminate all fun, and ignore them for 15-30 seconds. This shows that games necessitate polite teeth. Resume play once calm.

Use Taste Deterrents

Apply bitter apple spray onto areas of furniture or your body prone to puppy biting. Negative taste connections instruct what isn't ideal for the mouth.

Avoid Physical Corrections

Never strike, wrist flick, pinch, or scruff shake a growing puppy for biting behavior. This erodes trust in you and heightens detrimental defensive animosity that worsens long-term.

While mouthing eases by age 5-6 months naturally, rigorous teaching avoids harm in the meantime. Stay patient, consistent, and motivated towards soft habits.

Techniques for Handling Possessiveness

Guarding prized possessions, food bowls or resting areas can signal worry. Reinforce sharing and trade-offs using rewards:

Claim What's Yours

If kids grumble while taking something harmful away, say "Mine!" confidently. Then give something appealing in exchange, rewarding obedience. Teachers abandoning goods pays off.

Hand Feed Early On

Sit with a pup at mealtimes, adding delightful bits into the dish by hand randomly as they eat, with consent to touch their face and collar region frequently too. Reduces resource guarding.

Use Trading Games

Present delectable gifts while reaching carefully for stolen household belongings. Mark and reward allowing you to take the item, then return it marking again when they stop paying attention to receive it back.

Avoid Physical Takeaways

Stealing objects forcibly, threatening to hover close by, or sticking hands in bowls generally promotes possessive aggression. Always swap items instead of confrontation.

Teach Cue Words

Gradually pair the "Give" request with an opening palm to take objects, then "Take it" for returning goods, then "Leave it" for ignoring dropped items. These facilitate communication minimizing reactionary snapping.

While resource guarding is a deeply rooted instinct for guardian breeds like Mastiffs, thorough training based on relationships prevents escalations throughout adulthood. Stay proactive!

Chapter Nine

Exercise Requirements and Environmental Needs

Exercise Needs By Mastiff Life Stage

Providing adequate physical exercise levels maintains Mastiffs mentally and physically enriched without risking bone and joint injuries during maturation phases. Follow these age-based guidelines:

Puppyhood Up To 1 Year

Puppy exercise needs to focus on spontaneous play and training in soft grass, never forced running or climbing. Limit leashed walks to brief 10-minute introductions on level ground since stresses on building cartilage and ligaments overload immature joints. Socialization should take priority over cardio.

Adolescence up to 2 Years

Gradually extend leashed walks to 20-30 minutes max by this rapid growth period, allowing your pup to decide on pace and rest intervals. Continue off-leash play times in safe, enclosed places solely to maintain a steady state of cardio. Avoiding exertion, pace and constant nourishment encourages good muscular growth around the skeleton during this gangly stage.

Adulthood 2-6 Years

Twice daily 30-60 minute leashed walks are appropriate for physically mature individuals, complemented with yard play. Muscular fitness peaks over these years. Swimming and hiking build endurance if started gradually. Monitor for indicators of arthritis, hip dysplasia, or ligament difficulties.

Mature Adulthood 6 Years Onward

Lower intensity and tempo activities to a relaxing 20 minutes daily for older Mastiffs. Supplement walks with scent games, short toss fetch, and mild massage. Monitor for changes indicating osteoarthritis, cancer, or cardiac illness. Know when to step back and reduce expectations for elderly pets.

Check with your veterinarian about the optimal exercise program customized to your specific Mastiff's demands across life phases.

Playing, Walking, and Hiking With Your Mastiff Safely

Mastiffs appreciate trips outdoors with their family. Follow these safety rules for pleasurable adventures together at any age:

Mind the Heat

Overheating and dehydration are important hazards for big breeds. Bring water on hikes, stay in cooler morning/evening hours in summer, and take shade breaks. Avoid lengthy intensity trekking on hot pavement. Know indicators of heat exhaustion like heavy panting and bright red gums.

Prepare for Cold

Use dog jackets, booties, and paw wax in snow. Shorten winter walks and wipe paws entering to prevent ice build-up or salt discomfort. Avoid outdoor tie-outs in freezing temps.

Play Appropriate Games

Instead of jogging with a pup, opt for easy fetching activities retaining soft grass or sand footing. Encourage investigating different smells on relaxation walks to stimulate their imagination and wanderlust.

Walk Responsibly

Use front-attaching control harnesses and keep leash wraps on your hand. Refrain from retractable leashes that allow dashing after wildlife. Consider basket muzzles in on-leash situations if dog reactivity remains an issue. Follow leash laws strictly.

Mastiffs benefit from deliberate exercise tailored to the season and their age. Prioritize their comfort and safety while giving meaningful adventures.

Summer and Winter Weather Precautions

English Mastiffs require particular planning for temperature fluctuations due to their sensitive large breed health:

Preventing Overheating

Signs include:

- Excessive or loud panting
- Bright red gum color
- Increased salivation
- Dry heaving
- Weakness or difficulty to rise
- Elevated body temperature > 104°F

If these appear:

- Get dog indoors quickly

- Offer cool water sponge baths

- Place ice packs near neck and paws

- Provide new drinking water

- Seek emergency veterinary care if symptoms worsen or present with shock

Preventing Frostbite and Hypothermia

Signs include:

- Whimpers, trembling, lethargy
- Skin inside ears or gums turn bluish gray
- Paws feel inflamed or unpleasant from salt or ice contact

If these appear:

- Gently wash paws with lukewarm water
- Massage paws to restore circulation
- Cover with blanket dried fully
- Offer drinking warm water but not food yet

- Monitor for non-medical underlying causes such as arthritis discomfort

With modest adaptations, English Mastiffs can play safely in most weather situations. Pay attention to indicators of suffering and be ready to quit activities at first. Their health is the foremost priority with excessive hot or cold risks.

Chapter Ten

Grooming & General Care

Essentials

Coat Brushing, Nail, Dental and Ear Care

While grooming needs are moderate for short-haired Mastiffs, establishing handling routines minimizes uncomfortable veterinary visits and health difficulties down the road:

Target Shedding

Use a slicker brush monthly to remove loose hairs and distribute skin oils for a healthy coat. Brush against hair growth direction. Extra brushing helps reduce seasonal shedding surges.

Prevent Overgrown Nails

Trim tips monthly before they circle back towards paw pads using correctly sized clippers. Introduce handling paws early. Have a styptic powder on hand if you clip nails too short.

Daily Dental Care

Wipe outer teeth surfaces with gauze pads daily after eating. Weekly dental cleaning with dog-safe paste eliminates plaque buildup preventing periodontal disease that huge breeds are prone to.

Monitor Ears

Gently wipe inside ear flaps weekly checking for odor, discharge, or redness indicating infection. Pluck outside hair to facilitate air circulation. Never insert items deep into your ears.

Make at-home grooming positive from puppyhood up. Regular attention by owners helps Mastiffs accept handling when needing exams or treatment.

Bathing Techniques & Dry Shampooing

Though English Mastiffs don't require frequent full baths, practice these methods for fresh cleaning between deeper cleans:

Bathing Essentials

Before wet baths, comb shed hair, trim nails, and clean ears. Choose a dog-safe moisturizing shampoo and a non-slip bath mat. Use sprayer attachments avoiding ears and eyes. Rinse thoroughly to prevent skin irritation.

Dry Shampoo Options

Freshen up dirty coats between thorough baths by brushing in dry shampoo powder products, allowing it to sit 10 minutes before brushing out. Wipes also clean cheeks, paws, and surface dirt on bellies.

Post Bath Maintenance

Gently squeeze out water then cover in towels patting moisture, and avoid rough rubbing. Use a blow dryer on a low setting if they'll tolerate it. Brush again before the collar replaces the tags.

Limit Full Bath Frequency

Fully bathe every 6-8 weeks at most. Excess washing strips healthful vital oils from skin and fur. Spot clean dirty parts as needed between bathing.

With the correct shampoos, patience, and handling practices, bath periods can be a bonding plus grooming opportunity despite their big size.

Car & Plane Travel Tips

Travel takes forethought for big Mastiff breeds. Here are tips for smooth trips on the road and sky together:

Car Travel

Invest in a crash-test-rated crate or harness system holding your Mastiff safely during drives. Left loose they can create a severe projectile risk with hard braking. Provide non-spill dishes for drinking and no feeding at least one hour before departures. Pack toilet pads too.

Airplane Travel

Check airline mastiff size and weight restrictions for cabin or cargo rules. Choose direct flights under 5 hours wherever possible. Acclimate to crate dimensions beforehand. Freeze the dish inside providing ice for hydration as it melts. Attach "Live Animal" stickers with your contact details and "This Side Up" arrows on the crate. Ask the airline about temperature regulation procedures.

General Tips

Ensure the pet sitter has access to emergency contacts and veterinary records in case concerns arise when you're away. Bring health certificates while crossing state lines or national borders. Snap a snap pic of your pooch before departures in case separation arises. Mastiffs like vehicle journeys and experiences with their chosen people - with the appropriate preparation, travel creates lifelong memories!

Follow these Mastiff care, grooming, and handling practices to keep your canine buddy looking and feeling their best inside and out! Let me know if any part might benefit from extra expansion or specifics.

Chapter Eleven

Feeding & Nutrition Requirements

Caloric Needs By Life Stage

Rapidly expanding Mastiff puppies have different nutritional needs than adults to maintain bone, muscle, and organ growth without fat. Follow these changing guidelines:

8-12 Weeks Old

Weaned puppies need 4 scheduled meals of high-quality large-breed puppy formulation satisfying protein, fat, calcium, and calorie minimums for exponential increases. Around 700-800 calories stimulate development with meals based on expected adult size.

4-6 Months Old

Shift from 4 to 3 scheduled feedings when digesting capacities mature. Caloric demands peak at 4 months reaching 900-1400 calories daily for a 100+ pound adult breed. Control rapid growth by calculating accurate meals customized to weight gain goals.

6-18 Months Old

Reduce meals to twice daily feeding adult or large breed puppy compositions as the growth rate decelerates. Females achieve adult size around 12-15 months old, men at 18-24 months old. Adapt calories down if weight gain surpasses healthy curves.

Adulthood Through Senior Years

Twice daily feedings with total calories adequate for optimal condition, not maximal weight tolerances. Males above 100 pounds require 2000-3500 daily calories based on exercise levels and metabolism. Females in heat or lactating have greater demands. Senior dogs need fewer calories with lower activity.

Recommended Diets & Supplements

These additives improve joint health, bone density, and digestion:

All Life Stages Provide always accessible fresh clean water. Stainless steel non-tip bowls enable large breeds to drink sufficiently.

Puppy Diet

Feed all-life phases or large breed puppy formulation up to 18-24 months old, with a minimum of 22% protein, 12% fat, and controlled calcium under 1.5% levels.

Adult Diet Shift to maintenance formula with a minimum of 18% protein and 5% fat without the quick development acceleration of puppy feeds. Some intact guys thrive on more protein.

Joint Supplements Glucosamine, chondroitin, and fish oil promote cartilage cushioning and inflammatory regulation of bones/joints suffering much pressure from weight.

Probiotic Digestive Aids
Counteract gas while boosting absorption and stool quality.

Hydration Enhancers
Add water flavor enhancers promoting appropriate fluid consumption.

Veterinary guidance optimizes individual caloric goals across life periods. Supplements support entire body wellness enabled by personalized nutrition.

Preventing Bloat Risk

Giant deep-chested breeds like Mastiffs require preventatives to minimize deadly bloat and stomach twisting risk:

Understand Bloat

When the stomach expands with gas, food, or fluid, it can twist, shutting off apertures. This traps air and glasses causing great pain, shock, and fatality without quick treatment.

Feed Multiple Small Meals

Rather than one huge meal, divide daily calories into 2-3 smaller pieces allowing regular digestion across the day.

Slow Down Inhalation

Use puzzle toys hiding kibble inside rubber nubs. Ladle parts gradually into a snuffle mat. These force slower eating intake.

Avoid Vigorous Activity Before/After Eating Wait at least an hour following meals for intense playtime.

The jostling motion can contribute to trapped gasses.

Learn Emergency Signs

Unproductive retching, enlarged stomach, and distress signal vet emergency. Keep numbers handy. Surgery reduces pressure, allows stomach relocation, and enhances the odds of resisting shock.

While inherited factors contribute, owners have a crucial part in minimizing fatal bloat risk through intelligent food selections and calm routines surrounding feeding times for their Mastiff.

Chapter Twelve

Health & Medical Care

Recognizing Signs of Common Major Health Issues

Giant breeds like Mastiffs are prone to specific genetic conditions. Know what to watch for across life stages:

Orthopedic Disease

Lameness, difficulty standing, screaming when moving, and reluctance mounting stairs suggest possible hip dysplasia, arthritis, or elbow disorders needing veterinarian diagnostics. Meds ease discomfort.

Gastric Dilatation Volvulus

Unproductive retching and bloated, painful abdomen signal emergency GDV danger. Other indicators include restless pacing and abdominal distension. Requires prompt surgical intervention.

Osteosarcoma

Limping and later bone pain signifies this aggressive limb malignancy. It spreads swiftly but specific treatment protocols may slow down progression following amputation.

Mast Cell Tumors

These skin tumors mimic benign warts initially but often expand internally before physical problems manifest. Have new masses tested even if appearing harmless.

Cardiac Disease

Fatigue, fainting, or fluid buildup in the abdomen flags probable dilated cardiomyopathy. Annual tests screen high-risk breeds early to treat with drugs decreasing the onset of congestive heart failure.

Hypothyroidism

This frequent endocrine problem induces lethargy, obesity, and skin disorders. Annual checks identify thyroid hormone decreases addressed daily with oral supplementation restoring zest for life.

Catching conditions early increases comfort and longevity. Learn what's usual for your individual Mastiff to identify changes fast.

Budgeting for Healthcare Costs & Pet Insurance Options

Giant breeds suffer higher routine and emergency veterinary bills. Financially prepare with these tips:

Typical Preventative Care Annual Costs
- Physical exam & Vaccines: $200+
- Parasite Prevention: $150+

- Routine Diagnostics: $300+

- Dental Cleaning: $400+

- Monthly Supplements: $100+

Project Big Ticket Emergencies

- Bloat, toxin, or fracture surgery: $3,000+

- Cancer treatment: $5,000+

- ICU hospitalization stays $1,000+ per night

Pet Insurance Overview

- Lowers out-of-pocket expenditures considerably

- 90% reimbursement usual with $250 deductible - $60+/month premiums depending on age at enrolling

Compare multiple providers for optimum coverage. Sign puppies up early before prior condition exclusion periods. Review reimbursement procedures to grasp common and customary rate calculations. Save a "rainy day fund" for co-pays and deductibles too!

Adapting Home and Routine for Aging Dogs

Support older mastiffs (over age 7) to adjust to lower energy levels:

- Memory foam beds relieve arthritic joints overnight
- Ramps or steps assist going around securely
- Open kennels offer choice confinement as needed
- Massages increase circulation and bonding
- Mental games retain cognitive abilities
- Harnesses decrease strain on limping joints
- Raise food/water containers minimizing bend pressure
- Stick to familiar places and routines when possible
- Adapt outdoor toilet breaks for weaker mobility
- Increase lighting negotiating pathways
- Swap toys out for appropriate chew items

With simple adaptations to favor comfort and dignity, many Mastiffs enjoy several good years despite age-related changes. Focus on their quality of life and be ready to make the last humane call when more unpleasant days emerge than good.

20 homemade food recipe ideas for English Mastiff with ingredients and preparation instructions

Recipe 1: Beef and Sweet Potato Stew

Ingredients:

- 2 pounds lean ground beef

- 2 cups diced sweet potatoes

- 1 cup minced carrots

- 1 cup peas

 - 4 cups beef broth

- 1 tablespoon olive oil

Instructions:

1. In a big pot, heat olive oil over medium heat.

2. Add ground beef and sauté until browned, breaking it into small pieces with a spatula.

3. Add sweet potatoes, carrots, peas, and beef stock to the pot.

4. Bring the mixture to a boil, then reduce heat and simmer for 25-30 minutes until vegetables are cooked.

5. Allow the stew to cool before serving it to your English Mastiff.

Recipe 2: Chicken and Brown Rice Casserole

Ingredients:
- 3 lbs chicken thighs, boneless and skinless
- 2 cups brown rice
- 1 cup sliced zucchini
- 1 cup chopped spinach
- 4 cups chicken broth
- 2 tablespoons coconut oil

Instructions:
1. Preheat the oven to 375°F (190°C).

2. In a large baking dish, combine chicken thighs, brown rice, zucchini, spinach, chicken stock, and coconut oil.

3. Cover the dish with aluminum foil and bake for 45-50 minutes until the chicken is cooked through and the rice is soft.

4. Let the casserole cool somewhat before offering it to your English Mastiff.

Recipe 3: Turkey and Pumpkin Stew

Ingredients:

- 2 pounds minced turkey
- 1 can (15 oz) pumpkin puree
- 1 cup diced potatoes
- 1 cup chopped green beans
- 4 cups turkey or chicken broth
- 1 tablespoon coconut oil

Instructions:

1. In a big pot, heat coconut oil over medium heat.

2. Add ground turkey and heat until browned, breaking it into small pieces.

3. Stir in pumpkin puree, chopped potatoes, green beans, and broth.

4. Bring the mixture to a boil, then reduce heat and simmer for 20-25 minutes until potatoes are cooked through.

5. Allow the stew to cool before presenting it to your English Mastiff.

Recipe 4: Salmon and Quinoa Pilaf

Ingredients:

- 2 pounds fresh salmon filets, deboned

- 2 cups cooked quinoa

- 1 cup diced bell peppers

- 1 cup chopped broccoli

- 4 cups vegetable broth

- 2 teaspoons olive oil

Instructions:

1. Preheat the oven to 400°F (200°C).

2. Place salmon filets on a baking sheet lined with parchment paper and sprinkle with olive oil.

3. Bake for 15-20 minutes until salmon is cooked through and flakes readily with a fork.

4. In a large skillet, heat olive oil over medium heat.

5. Add cooked quinoa, bell peppers, broccoli, and vegetable broth to the skillet.

6. Cook for 10-12 minutes until vegetables are soft.

7. Flake the cooked fish and gently incorporate it into the quinoa pilaf.

8. Let the pilaf cool before presenting it to your English Mastiff.

Recipe 5: Lamb and Barley Stew

Ingredients:
- 2 lbs lamb stew meat, cubed
- 1 cup pearl barley
- 1 cup diced butternut squash
- 1 cup chopped kale
- 4 cups beef broth
- 2 teaspoons butter

Instructions:

1. In a large pot, melt butter over medium heat.

2. Add lamb stew meat and heat until browned on all sides.

3. Stir in pearl barley, butternut squash, kale, and beef broth.

4. Bring the mixture to a boil, then reduce heat and simmer for 45-50 minutes until the lamb is cooked.

5. Allow the stew to cool before presenting it to your English Mastiff.

Recipe 6: Pork and Potato Hash

Ingredients:

- 2 pounds ground pork

- 2 cups diced potatoes

- 1 cup chopped celery

- 1 cup peas

- 4 cups pork or vegetable broth

- 2 teaspoons coconut oil

Instructions:

1. In a large skillet, heat coconut oil over medium heat.

2. Add ground pork and sauté until browned, breaking it into small pieces.

3. Stir in diced potatoes, celery, peas, and broth.

4. Cook for 20-25 minutes until potatoes are cooked and the mixture has thickened.

5. Let the hash cool before offering it to your English Mastiff.

Recipe 7: Venison and Lentil Stew

Ingredients:

- 2 lbs venison stew meat, cubed
- 2 cups dried green lentils
- 1 cup diced carrots
- 1 cup chopped tomatoes
- 4 cups beef or venison broth
- 2 teaspoons olive oil

Instructions:

1. In a big pot, heat olive oil over medium heat.

2. Add venison stew meat and heat until browned on all sides.

3. Stir in dried lentils, carrots, tomatoes, and broth.

4. Bring the mixture to a boil, then reduce heat and simmer for 1 hour until the venison is soft and the lentils are cooked.

5. Allow the stew to cool before presenting it to your English Mastiff.

Recipe 8: Duck and Rice Congee

Ingredients:
- 2 pounds duck breast, skinless
- 2 cups white rice
- 1 cup sliced carrots
- 1 cup chopped bok choy
- 4 cups duck or chicken broth
- 2 tablespoons sesame oil

Instructions:
1. In a large pot, heat sesame oil over medium heat.

2. Add duck breast and heat until browned on both sides.

3. Stir in white rice, carrots, bok choy, and broth.

4. Bring the mixture to a boil, then reduce heat and simmer for 45-50 minutes until the rice is mushy and the duck is cooked through.

5. Shred the cooked duck and put it back into the congee.

6. Let the congee cool before offering it to your English Mastiff.

Recipe 9: Rabbit and Potato Stew

Ingredients:
- 2 lbs rabbit meat, deboned and cubed
- 2 cups diced potatoes
- 1 cup chopped onions
- 1 cup sliced mushrooms
- 4 cups vegetable broth
- 2 tablespoons butter

Instructions:

1. In a large pot, melt butter over medium heat.

2. Add rabbit meat and heat until browned on all sides.

3. Stir in diced potatoes, onions, mushrooms, and broth.

4. Bring the mixture to a boil, then decrease heat and simmer for 30-35 minutes until the rabbit is soft and the potatoes are cooked through.

5. Allow the stew to cool before presenting it to your English Mastiff.

Recipe 10: Sardine and Vegetable Medley

Ingredients:

- 4 cans (3.75 oz each) of sardines in water, drained
- 2 cups boiled barley
- 1 cup sliced bell peppers (assorted hues)
- 1 cup sliced asparagus
- 1 cup grated carrots
- 2 tablespoons olive oil

Instructions:

1. In a large skillet, heat olive oil over medium heat.

2. Add diced bell peppers, asparagus, and grated carrots.

3. Cook for 8-10 minutes until vegetables are soft.

4. Stir in cooked barley and sardines, breaking them into smaller pieces.

5. Cook for an additional 2-3 minutes until heated through.

6. Let the mixture cool before offering it to your English Mastiff.

Recipe 11: Bison and Sweet Potato Casserole

Ingredients:
- 2 pounds ground bison
- 2 cups diced sweet potatoes
- 1 cup minced green beans
- 1 cup sliced apples
- 4 cups beef or bison broth
- 2 tablespoons coconut oil

Instructions:

1. Preheat the oven to 375°F (190°C).

2. In a skillet, heat coconut oil over medium heat.

3. Add ground bison and heat until browned.

4. In a large baking dish, combine cooked bison, sweet potatoes, green beans, apples, and broth.

5. Cover with foil and bake for 45-50 minutes until sweet potatoes are cooked.

6. Let the casserole cool before offering it to your English Mastiff.

Recipe 12: Lamb and Lentil Stew

Ingredients:
- 2 lbs lamb shoulder, cubed
- 2 cups dried brown lentils
- 1 cup diced butternut squash
- 1 cup chopped Swiss chard
- 4 cups lamb or veggie broth
- 2 teaspoons olive oil

Instructions:
1. In a big pot, heat olive oil over medium heat.

2. Add lamb shoulder and heat until browned on all sides.

3. Stir in dried lentils, butternut squash, Swiss chard, and broth.

4. Bring to a boil, then reduce heat and simmer for 1 hour until lamb is tender and lentils are cooked.

5. Allow the stew to cool before presenting it to your English Mastiff.

Recipe 13: Turkey and Pumpkin Meatballs

Ingredients:
- 2 pounds ground turkey
- 1 cup pumpkin puree
- 1 cup rolled oats
- 1/2 cup grated Parmesan cheese
- 2 eggs
- 2 teaspoons chopped parsley

Instructions:
1. Preheat the oven to 375°F (190°C).

2. In a large bowl, add ground turkey, pumpkin puree, rolled oats, Parmesan cheese, eggs, and parsley.

3. Roll the mixture into meatballs and set them on a baking sheet lined with parchment paper.

4. Bake for 25-30 minutes until cooked thoroughly.

5. Let the meatballs cool before presenting them to your English Mastiff.

Recipe 14: Chicken and Barley Soup

Ingredients:

- 3 pounds chicken thighs, boneless and skinless
- 2 cups pearl barley
- 1 cup diced carrots
- 1 cup chopped celery
- 4 cups chicken broth
- 2 teaspoons olive oil

Instructions:

1. In a big pot, heat olive oil over medium heat.

2. Add chicken thighs and sauté until browned.

3. Stir in pearl barley, carrots, celery, and broth.

4. Bring to a boil, then decrease heat and simmer for 45-50 minutes until chicken is cooked through and barley is soft.

5. Allow the soup to cool before presenting it to your English Mastiff.

Recipe 15: Fish and Quinoa Patties

Ingredients:

- 2 lbs white fish filets (such as cod or haddock), deboned
- 2 cups cooked quinoa
- 1 cup grated zucchini
- 1/2 cup minced cilantro
- 2 eggs
- 1 tablespoon lemon juice

Instructions:

1. Preheat the oven to 375°F (190°C) and line a baking sheet with parchment paper.

2. In a food processor, pulse fish filets until finely chopped.

3. Transfer chopped fish to a large bowl and add cooked quinoa, grated zucchini, cilantro, eggs, and lemon juice. Mix until well blended.

4. Shape the mixture into patties and set them on the prepared baking sheet.

5. Bake for 20-25 minutes until patties are cooked through and golden brown.

6. Let the patties cool before offering them to your English Mastiff.

Recipe 16: Venison and Potato Skillet

Ingredients:
- 2 lbs venison steak, thinly sliced
- 2 cups diced potatoes
- 1 cup chopped bell peppers (assorted colors)
- 1 cup sliced onions
- 4 cloves garlic, minced
- 2 tablespoons olive oil
- Salt and pepper to taste

Instructions:

1. Heat olive oil in a large skillet over medium-high heat.

2. Add sliced venison steak and heat until browned, about 5-7 minutes.

3. Add diced potatoes, chopped bell peppers, sliced onions, and minced garlic to the skillet.

4. Season with salt and pepper to taste.

5. Cook for a further 10-12 minutes, turning periodically, until the potatoes are soft and the vegetables are cooked.

6. Allow the skillet to cool slightly before serving it to your English Mastiff.

Recipe 17: Pork and Pumpkin Stir-Fry

Ingredients:

- 2 lbs pork tenderloin, thinly sliced
- 1 cup pumpkin puree
- 1 cup sliced mushrooms
- 1 cup sliced zucchini

- 1 cup shredded cabbage

- 2 teaspoons soy sauce

- 2 teaspoons sesame oil - 1 tablespoon honey

Instructions:

1. In a large wok or skillet, heat sesame oil over medium-high heat.

2. Add sliced pork tenderloin and heat until browned, about 5-7 minutes.

3. Stir in pumpkin puree, sliced mushrooms, sliced zucchini, shredded cabbage, soy sauce, and honey.

4. Cook for a further 5-7 minutes, turning regularly, until the veggies are soft and the pork is cooked through.

5. Allow the stir-fry to cool somewhat before presenting it to your English Mastiff.

Recipe 18: Chicken and Rice Meatloaf

Ingredients:

- 3 lbs shredded chicken

- 2 cups cooked brown rice

- 1 cup diced carrots

- 1 cup chopped broccoli

- 1 cup grated Parmesan cheese

- 2 eggs

- 1/4 cup tomato sauce

Instructions:

1. Preheat the oven to 375°F (190°C) and grease a loaf pan.

2. In a large bowl, add ground chicken, cooked brown rice, sliced carrots, chopped broccoli, grated Parmesan cheese, eggs, and tomato sauce.

3. Mix until completely blended.

4. Transfer the mixture to the prepared loaf pan and distribute it evenly.

5. Bake for 45-50 minutes until cooked through and golden brown on top.

6. Allow the meatloaf to cool before slicing and presenting it to your English Mastiff.

Recipe 19: Lamb and Lentil Curry

Ingredients:

- 2 lbs lamb leg meat, cubed

- 2 cups dry green lentils

- 1 cup diced tomatoes

- 1 cup chopped onions

- 1 cup coconut milk

- 2 teaspoons curry powder

- 2 tablespoons olive oil

- Salt and pepper to taste

Instructions:

1. In a big pot, heat olive oil over medium heat.

2. Add cubed lamb leg meat and heat until browned on all sides.

3. Stir in dried green lentils, diced tomatoes, chopped onions, coconut milk, and curry powder.

4. Season with salt and pepper to taste.

5. Bring to a boil, then reduce heat and simmer for 1 hour until the lamb is tender and the lentils are done.

6. Allow the dish to cool slightly before offering it to your English Mastiff.

Recipe 20: Fish and Vegetable Chowder

Ingredients:

- 2 lbs white fish filets (such as cod or halibut), diced

- 2 cups sliced potatoes - 1 cup chopped carrots

- 1 cup chopped celery - 1 cup frozen corn kernels

- 4 cups fish or veggie broth - 2 tablespoons butter

- 1/2 cup heavy cream

Instructions:

1. In a large pot, melt butter over medium heat.

2. Add diced potatoes, chopped carrots, chopped celery, and frozen corn kernels to the saucepan.

3. Cook for 5-7 minutes until vegetables are slightly softened.

4. Stir in fish broth and bring to a simmer.

5. Add cubed fish filets to the pot and boil for 8-10 minutes until the fish is cooked through.

6. Stir in heavy cream and boil for an additional 2-3 minutes.

7. Allow the chowder to cool slightly before presenting it to your English Mastiff.